CHINESE PAPER-CUT

CHINESE ZODIAC STORY THEATRE

中國剪紙藝術

Origin and history

Chinese paper-cutting originated from the activities of ancient ancestors and was a traditional part of Chinese culture. Before the invention of paper, people used other thin materials, such as leaves, silver foil, silk and even leather, to engrave the hollow pattern. Later, when paper was invented, people realized that the material was easy to cut, store and discard, and paper became the main material for such art.

For more than a thousand years, people (mainly women) have been cutting paper as part of their leisure activities. Folk paper-cutting spreads a wider range and has a rich artistic expression. Paper-cuts are used to decorate doors, windows and walls to show happiness and festivals.

Paper-cut past and present is mainly used to express people's hopes, gratitude and other emotional decorations or aesthetics.
Cut a piece of red paper with a pair of scissors, and the paper cut is given a simple but exaggerated beauty. The vividly depicted paper cuts have different meanings.

【起源和历史】

中国剪纸起源於古代祭祀祖先的活动，是中国文化的传统部分。
在纸张发明之前，人们使用其他薄的材料，
如树叶，银箔，丝绸甚至皮革，来雕刻镂空图案。
后来，当纸张被发明时，
人们意识到这种材料易於切割，存储和丢弃，
纸张成为这类艺术品的主要材料。

一千多年来，人们（主要是女性）一直在剪纸
作为休闲活动的一部分。
民间剪纸传播范围更广，具有丰富的艺术表现力。
剪纸被用来装饰门，窗和墙壁，以显示快乐和节日。

剪纸过去和现在主要用于表达人们的希望，
感恩和其他情感的装饰或美学方式。
用一把剪刀切开一张红纸，
剪纸被赋予了简单但夸张的美感。
生动描绘的剪纸具有不同的含义。

Paper cutting steps

1. Photocopy or print out the produced sample
2. Fold the colored paper into the way needed for paper cutting
3. Fix the sample to the colored paper with glue, stapler or paper clip
4. Follow the paper-cutting techniques to cut paper or carve

Paper-cutting tools

1. **Colored paper:**
   Thin paper：Need to fold many times.
   Thick Paper：Need to hang when done.

2. **Scissors:**
   Medium size：Cutout and large area digging.
   Small scissors：Cut details.

3. **Knife:**
   Use a utility knife and pen knife to go in the direction of the hand
   Carved from top to bottom, left to right.

【剪纸步骤】

1. 把制作的样稿影印或打印出来
2. 将色纸折成剪纸需要的方式
3. 以胶水、钉书机或回纹针将样稿固定在色纸上
4. 依照剪纸技巧来剪纸或雕刻

【剪纸工具】

1. 色纸：
   薄纸-需要折很多次的技巧
   厚纸-完成後需要吊饰悬挂
2. 剪刀：
   中等大小-剪出轮廓与大面积挖孔
   小剪刀-剪细节处
3. 小刀：
   使用美工刀货笔刀，顺著手的方向
   由上往下，由左往右刻

Paper-cutting skills

1. Circular: expresses circular patterns such as flowers and eyes.
2. Crescent shape: expresses the smooth curves of characters' eyebrows, petals, etc.
3. Zigzag: expressing the hair of characters and animals.
4. Square: express doors and windows, buildings, utensils, text.
5. Curve: the outline of the paper-cut theme, there is no fixed direction, mainly smooth lines.

Scissors and knife engraving
1. Draw a sketch first and make a cut
2. Carve with a knife, do not turn the knife when turning
3. Turn the paper, the curve can be more prominent and smooth

【剪纸技巧】

1. 圆形：表现花朵、眼睛等圆形图案
2. 月牙形：表现人物眉毛、花瓣等圆滑的曲线
3. 锯齿形：表现人物、动物的毛发
4. 方形：表现门窗、建筑、器物、文字
5. 曲线形：表现剪纸题材的轮廓，没有固定的方向，以流畅线条为主

剪刀和刀刻，即剪镂刀刻两种
1. 先画稿，标示剪去和留下的地方
2. 用刀刻，转弯的时候不转刀
3. 转纸，曲线更能突出及流畅

Small theater assembly【小剧场组装】

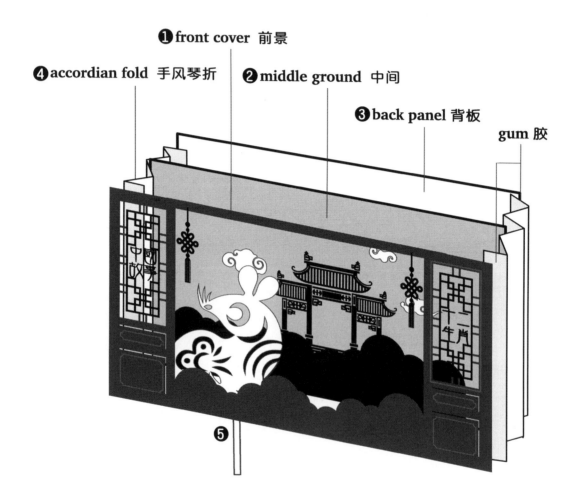

There are many viewers, which can be enlarged according to the size and proportion.
观赏人数多，可以依照尺寸等比例放大制作

❶ Black paper cutout 黑色纸镂空 — 42cm × 21cm

Red backing paper 红色底纸

gum 胶

❷ Black paper cutou 黑色纸镂空

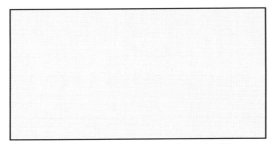

❸ White thick paper 白色厚纸

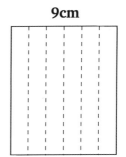

❹ Thick paper 厚纸 — 9cm

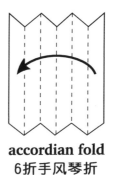

accordian fold
6折手风琴折

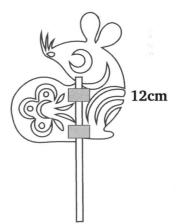

12cm

❺ Yellow paper cutoutc 黄色纸镂空
Stick stick 黏贴棍棒

THE RACE STORY OF CHINESE ZODIAC ANIMALS

The story is about the race between the animals. Chinese legend said that the Jade Emperor, who was the ruler of the heavens, asked all the animals to participate his birthday (on the ninth day of the first Chinese lunar month) and held a great race. The first 12 animals that came could be given a place in the calendar.

As soon as the cat heard the news, he asked the rat to wake him up on the morning . The rat promised to do so. But he went out early without waking up the cat on that day.

Although the rat got up early and run fast, he became worried when he arrived at the river bank as he was a poor swimmer. After waiting for the come of the ox, he asked the help from the ox to carry him across the river. With the help of the honest and helpful ox, the rat successfully crossed the river. However, he didn't jump off from the ox's back until they arrived at the door of the Jade Emperor. Just as the ox was about to win the race, the rat leapt to the Jade Emperor before the ox. Thus, the rat won the first place in the race and the second the ox. Later came the Tiger, Rabbit, Dragon, Snake, Horse, Sheep, Monkey, Rooster, and Dog. The lazy pig arrived last and got the last place.

The cat, on the tenth day of the first lunar month woke up early and hurried on his journey. When he came to the heaven, other animals all mocked him that he had arrived one day later. From then on, the cat and rat became enemies. Every time the cat meets the rat, he would chase and try to eat the rat.

【中国十二生肖的故事】

这个故事是关於动物之间的竞赛。中国传说提到,天上的统治者玉皇大帝邀请所有动物参加他的生日(农历正月初九),并举行了一场盛大的比赛。可以为前12只动物指定在日历中地位。

猫一听到这个消息,就请老鼠早上叫醒他。老鼠答应了。但是它那天很早就出去了,没有把猫叫醒。

尽管这只老鼠起得很早并且跑得很快,但它还是不擅於游泳,到河岸时却感到担心。在等待牛的到来之後,他请求牛的帮助将他带过河。在诚实和乐於助人的牛的帮助下,老鼠成功地渡过了河。但是当它们到达玉皇大帝的门前,它才从牛背上跳下来。当牛正要赢得比赛时,老鼠在牛之前跳到了玉皇大帝前。因此,老鼠在比赛中赢得第一名,第二名是牛。後来出现了虎,兔,龙,蛇,马,羊,猴,公鸡和狗。懒猪最後到达得到了最後一席。

猫在农历正月初十很早就醒来,匆匆赶去。当它来到天堂时,其它动物都笑它最后一天到达。从那以後,猫和老鼠成了敌人。每当猫遇到老鼠时,他都会追逐并吃掉老鼠。

About the stories and legends related to zodiac signs , there are many versions. This is well known and easy for children to understand.

关於与十二生肖有关的故事和传说,有很多版本。这是众所周知的,孩子们很容易理解。

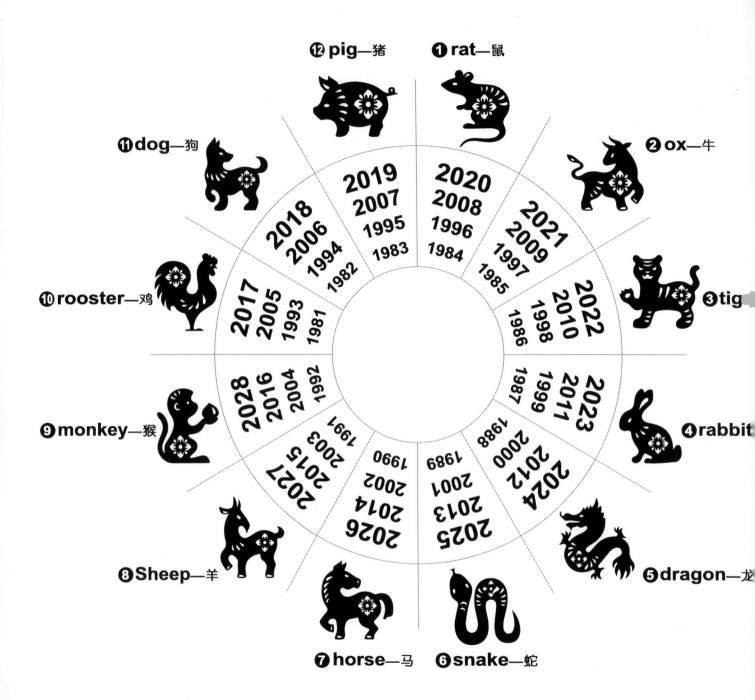

Chinese Zodiac：

There are zodiac signs in China, arranged in the following order: rat, cx, tiger, rabbit, dragon, snake, horse, Sheep, monkey, rooster, dog, pig.

In traditional Chinese culture, every 12 years is a reincarnation. In ancient times, Chinese people worshipped animals, so people used twelve animals to represent each year. These animals were called zodiac signs, and the zodiac signs appeared in a fixed order.

Find your zodiac animal and learn more.

十二生肖：

中国有十二生肖，按以下顺序排列：

鼠，牛，虎，兔，龙，蛇，马，羊，猴，公鸡，狗，猪。

在中国传统文化里，每十二年是一个轮回。

古时候的中国人很崇拜动物，所以人们用十二种动物代表每一年，这些动物被称为十二生肖，十二生肖按照固定的顺序出现。

找到你的生肖动物，并了解更多信息。

Animal	Shichen	Time Period	Animal Features during the Period
Rat	Zi-子	23:00-01:00	Rats are most active during this period in seeking food.
Ox	Chou-丑	01:00-03:00	Oxen ruminate slowly and leisurely.
Tiger	Yin-寅	03:00-05:00	Tigers are most ferocious and hurt prey more.
Rabbit	Mao-卯	05:00-07:00	The jade rabbit on the moon is busy pounding medicinal herb according to the tale.
Dragon	Chen-辰	07:00-09:00	Dragons are hovering in the sky to give rainfall.
Snake	Si-巳	09:00-11:00	Snakes start to leave their caves.
Horse	Wu-午	11:00-13:00	The sun is overhead. Other animals are lying down for a rest, while Horses are still standing.
Sheep	Wei-未	13:00-15:00	Sheep(Goats) eat grass and urinate frequently.
Monkey	Shen-申	15:00-17:00	Monkeys are screeching and most lively.
Rooster	You-酉	17:00-19:00	Roosters return to their coops as it is getting dark.
Dog	Xu-戌	19:00-21:00	Dogs are most alert and begin to do their duty to guard houses.
Pig	Hai-亥	21:00-23:00	Pigs are sleeping soundly and growing fast.

Chinese Zodiac and Time (Shichen):

"Shichen" is a timing unit in ancient China and an old Chinese way of dividing a day. Based on the time of sun rise, the traditional Chinese people divided a day which has 24 hours into 12 segments. These segments with each having two hours are called Shichen. Each two-hour period (one Shichen) is given the name of one of the 12 Earthly Branches.

By observing life characters of animals in different time periods, the Chinese people linked each Shichen with one of the twelve Chinese zodiac animals.

The picture on the left is the connection between the zodiac and the hour:

12个生肖和时间（时辰）：

"时辰"是中国古代的计时单位，是中国古代的分时方式。根据太阳升起的时间，传统的中国人将一天分为12时段。每个时段都有两个小时，称为"时辰"。每两个小时(1个时辰)被命为12个地分支之一。

透过观察不同时期动物的生活特徵，中国人将每只时辰与十二种生肖之一联系起来。

左图是生肖与时辰之间的联系：

【Zodiac Animal—Rat】

shu

甲骨文

金文
篆体

Personality Traits：
Quick-witted, resourceful, versatile, kind

Recent Years of the Rat：
1948, 1960, 1972, 1984, 1996, 2008, 2020

celebrity：
William Shakespeare, George Washington

Best match:
dragon, monkey, cow

人格特质：
机智、资源丰富、多才多艺、善良

近年来的老鼠：
1948(2.10), 1960(1.28), 1972(2.15), 1984(2.2), 1996(2.19), 2008(2.7), 2020(1.25)

名人：
威廉·莎士比亚、乔治·华盛顿

最佳搭配：
龙、猴、牛

【Zodiac Animal—Ox】

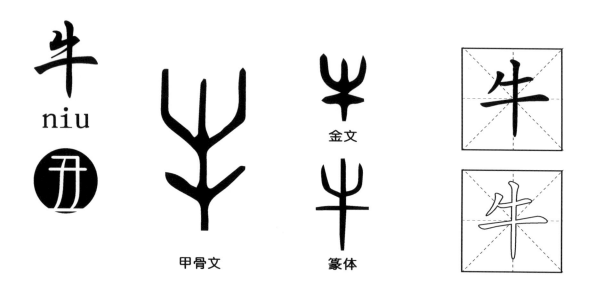

Personality Traits:
Diligent, dependable, strong, determined

Recent Years of the Ox:
1949, 1961, 1973, 1985, 1997, 2009, 2021

celebrity:
William Shakespeare, George Washington

Best matches:
rat, snake, rooster

个性:
勤奋、可靠、坚强、坚定

近年来的牛:
1949（1.29）,1961（2.15）,1973（2.3）,1985（2.20）
1997（2.7）,2009（1.26）,2021（2.12）

名人:
拿破仑、文森特、梵高

最佳匹配:
鼠、蛇、鸡

【Zodiac Animal—Tiger】

甲骨文

金文
篆体

Personality Traits:
Brave,confident,stubborn,competitive

Recent Years of the Tiger:
1950,1962,1974,1986,1998,2010,2022

celebrity:
marco polo,Marilyn Monroe

Best matches:
horse, dog

个性：
勇敢、自信、倔强、有竞争力

近年来的虎：
1950（2.17）,1962（2.5）,1974（1.23）,1986（2.9）
1998（1.28）,2010（2.14）,2022（2.1）

名人：
马可波罗、玛丽莲梦露

最佳匹配：
马、狗

【Zodiac Animal—Rabbit】

Personality Traits：
elegant,kind,responsible,shy

Recent Years of the Rabbit：
1951,1963,1975,1987,1999,2011,2023

celebrity：
confucius,albert einstein

Best matches:
Sheep, pig, dog

个性：
优雅、善良、负责任、害羞

近年来的兔：
1951(2.6),1963(1.25),1975(2.11),1987(1.29),
1999(2.16),2011(2.3),2023(1.22)

名人：
孔子、艾尔伯特爱因斯坦

最佳匹配：
绵羊、猪、狗

【Zodiac Animal—Dragon】

long

甲骨文

金文

篆体

Personality Traits：
Confident, intelligent, enthusiastic, perfectionist

Recent Years of the Dragon：
1952,1964,1976,1988,2000,2012,2024

celebrity：
Bruce Lee, sigmund freud

Best matches:
rat, monkey, rooster

个性：
自信、聪明、热情、完美主义者

近年来的龙：
1952(1.27)、1964(2.13)、1976(1.31)、1988(2.17)
2000(2.5)、2012(1.23)、2024(2.10)

名人：
李小龙、西格蒙德、弗洛伊德

最佳匹配：
鼠、猴、鸡

【Zodiac Animal—Hsnake】

she

甲骨文

金文

篆体

Personality Traits:
intelligent, active, energetic, independent

Recent Years of the Hsnake:
1953,1965,1977,1989,2001,2013,2025

celebrity:
chopin, teddy roosevelt

Best matches:
tiger, sheep, dog

个性：
智能、活跃、精力充沛、独立

近年来的蛇：
1953（2.14）,1965（2.2）,1977（2.18）,1989（2.6）
2001（1.24）,2013（2.10）,2025（1.29）

名人：
肖邦、泰迪罗斯福

最佳匹配：
老虎、绵羊、狗

【Zodiac Animal—Horse】

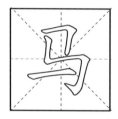

甲骨文 篆体 金文

Personality Traits：
Enigmatic,wise,Peace,humor

Recent Years of the Horse：
1954,1966,1978,1990,2002,2014,2026

celebrity：
charles darwin,abraham lincoln

Best matches:
ox, rooster, tiger

个性：
神秘、明智、平和、幽默感

近年来的马：
1954（2.3）,1966（1.21）,1978（2.7）,1990（1.27）
2002（2.12）,2014（1.31）,2026（2.17）

名人：
查尔斯·达尔文、亚伯拉罕·林肯

最佳匹配：
牛、鸡、虎

【Zodiac Animal—Sheep】

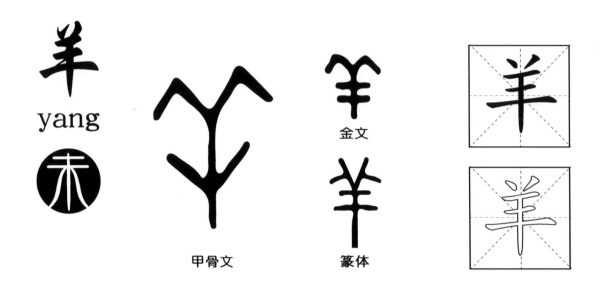

Personality Traits：
Calm,gentle,sympathetic,courtesy

Recent Years of the Sheep：
1955,1967,1979,1991,2003,2015,2027

celebrity：
Michelangelo,mark Twain

Best matches:
rabbit, horse, pig

个性：
冷静、温柔、同情、礼貌

近年来的羊：
1955(1.24),1967(2.9),1979(1.28),1991(2.15)
2003(2.1),2015(2.19),2027(2.7)

名人：
米开朗基罗、马克吐温

最佳搭配：
兔子、马、猪

【Zodiac Animal—Monkey】

hou

甲骨文

金文

篆体

Personality Traits:
Sharp,smart,curiosity,creativity

Recent Years of the Monkey:
1956,1968,1980,1992,2004,2016,2028

celebrity:
julius caesar,leonardo da vinci

Best match:
rat, dragon, snake

个性：
敏锐、聪明、好奇、创造力

近年来的猴：
1956(2.12)、1968(1.30)、1980(2.16)、1992(2.4)
2004(1.22)、2016(2.8)、2028(1.26)

名人：
凯撒大帝、莱昂纳多达芬奇

最佳搭配：
鼠、龙、蛇

【Zodiac Animal—Rooster】

甲骨文

金文

篆体

Personality Traits:
loyal, honest, prudent

Recent Years of the Rooster:
1957, 1969, 1981, 1993, 2005, 2017, 2029

celebrity:
benjamin franklin, george gershwin

Best match:
tiger, rabbit, horse

个性:
忠诚、诚实、谨慎

近年来的公鸡:
1957(1.31)、1969(2.17)、1981(2.5)、1993(1.23)
2005(2.9)、2017(1.28)、2029(2.13)

名人:
本杰明·富兰克林、温斯顿丘吉尔

最佳搭配:
虎、兔、马

【Zodiac Animal—Dog】

gou

甲骨文

金文

篆体

Personality Traits：
Observant,hardworking,shrewd,outspoken

Recent Years of the Dog：
1958,1970,1982,1994,2006,2018,2030

celebrity：
Britney Spears,Roger Federer

Best matches:
Ox, dragon, snake

个性：
细心、勤奋、精明、直言不讳

近年来的狗：
1958(2.18),1970(2.6),1982(1.25),1994(2.10)
2006(1.29),2018(2.16),2030(2.2)

名人：
布兰妮斯皮尔斯、罗杰费德勒

最佳搭配：
牛、龙、蛇

【Zodiac Animal—Pig】

zhu

甲骨文 篆体

金文

Personality Traits:
sincere, Compassionate, generous, diligent

Recent Years of the Pig:
1959,1971,1983,1995,2007,2019,2031

celebrity:
ernest hemingway, Arnold Schwarzenegger

Best match:
sheep, rabbit

个性：
真诚、同情心、慷慨、勤奋

近年来的猪：
1959(2.8),1971(1.27),1983(2.13),1995(1.31)
2007(2.18),2019(2.5),2031(1.23)

名人：
海明威、阿诺德施瓦辛格

最佳搭配：
羊、兔

CHINESE PAPER-CUT

Inscribed in 2009 on the Representative List of the Intangible Cultural Heritage of Humanity

© 2008 Shaanxi culture Department

Present throughout China and in various ethnic groups, paper-cut is a popular art integral to everyday lives. A predominantly female pursuit, it is transmitted from mother to daughter over a long period of time, beginning in childhood, and is particularly common in rural areas. It earns the most skilful artists respect and admiration. Many techniques are used: the paper can be cut or engraved with a chisel, coloured or left blank. Increasingly, modern technologies are used. Motifs, which vary greatly and are often devised by the artist, depend on the region of origin (for example, in southern China fine and delicate motifs predominate) and the purpose of the product, which might be used for interior decor (windows, beds and ceilings), festivities (weddings, birthdays and ceremonies), or prayers (invoking the rain, warding off the devil, and so on). As a key part of Chinese social life in all ethnic groups, paper-cut expresses the moral principles, philosophies and aesthetic ideals of its exponents. It continues to provide an outlet for emotion and is experiencing an unprecedented revival.

2009年列入人类非物质文化遗产代表作名录

© 2008陕西省文化厅

剪纸存在中国各地和各个民族,是日常生活中不可或缺的一种流行艺术。它主要是女性的追求,从童年开始就长期由母亲传到女儿,在农村地区尤其普遍。赢得最熟练的艺术家尊重和钦佩。使用许多技术:可以用凿子将纸切割或雕刻,著色或留空。越来越多地区使用现代技术。图案富有变化,通常由艺术家设计,取决於原产地(例如在中国南方,精美细腻的图案占主导地位)和可用於室内装饰(窗,床和天花板),庆祝活动(婚礼,生日和仪式)或祈祷(吸引雨水,抵御魔鬼等等)。剪纸作为各民族中国社会生活的重要组成,表达了道德信念,哲学和审美观念。它继续为情感提供出口,并且正在经历前所未有的复兴。

Printed in Great Britain
by Amazon